Praise for the P

Bill Brown's poems are lyrically, inescapably stories—stories that come from one man's slow, attentive walk through his world, asking, listening close, stopping to pry things up for what's underneath.

    —*Peter Stillman,* Proof of Passage

Like Gustav Mahler's music, Bill Brown's poems offer us voices rich in passion and intensity. Brown opens us up to energies of this earth, both bright and dark, illuminating and sinister.

    —*Malcolm Glass,* Mirrors, Myths and Dreams

Brown's poems have a sharply imagistic quality, almost painterly in effect, brilliant and definitive almost as color itself.

    —*George Scarbrough,* Under the Lemon Tree

And it truly is the lucky reader who is indebted to Brown's determination to hold onto and to shine his unique and masterful light upon all he loves or has ever loved. Brown's deeply felt and exquisitely crafted poems are informed by many powerful traditions and landscapes.

    —*Cathy Smith Bowers,* The Collected Poems of Cathy Smith Bowers

Also by Bill Brown

Holding On By Letting Go
(1986)

Important Words, A Book for Poets and Writers
(1991)

What the Night Told Me
(1992)

The Art of Dying
(1996)

Gods of Little Pleasures
(2001)

Yesterday's Hay
(2005)

Tatters
(2007)

Late Winter
(2008)

The News Inside
(2010)

Elemental
(2014)

Morning Window
(2017)

THE CAIRNS

THE CAIRNS

For Norma —

POEMS

New and Selected

Cairns Mark the Way —

Bill Brown

Peace / Hope —

Bill Brown

1/19

3

THREE: A TAOS PRESS

Copyright © 2018 by Bill Brown

All rights reserved

First U.S. edition 2018

No part of this book may be used or reproduced in any form by any means, electronic or mechanical, including photocopying, recording, or any information storage and retrieval system, without prior written permission from the author, artist, galleries, museums, estates, and publishers.

Book Design & Typesetting: Lesley Cox, FEEL Design Associates, Taos, NM

Press Logo Design: William Watson, Castro Watson, New York, NY

Author Photograph: Suzanne C. Brown, Greenbrier, TN

Text Typeset in Minion Pro and Gotham

Printed in the United States of America by Cottrell Printing Company

ISBN: 978-0-9994848-0-7

P.O. Box 370627
Denver, CO 80237.
www.3taospress.com

10 9 8 7 6 5 4 3 2 1

With loving affection, this book is dedicated to
my siblings Geron, Clark, and Clay
to my sister-in-law Jenny
and most of all, to my wife Suzanne—without her strong
support, these books never would have been written.

Thank you to Andrea Watson whose sharp eye
helped me to shape this collection.

The Cairns

They're stacked beside the creek
on a hidden gravel road—patience
and craft, the artful searching,

seeing, chipping, shaping. Mostly
limestone, each rock—millions of years
forming, fossilized, story-filled—itself a cairn.

The hours spent in rugged contemplation,
water burble, wind in leaves, the forest's sway—
a present for those who pass as the earth

crumbles in time what human hands have made.
I stack words to remember what words alone
can't say. *The tongue is an eye*, a poet wrote,

not just a choking muscle, fumbling with age.
The earth a grave of lost words, stones
and children's bones; a cairn, itself, crude and holey.

The gift is in the labor, mother taught—
scraped palms, broken nails, tired backs,
the ordered wonder of shape.

Contents

THE CAIRNS

NEW POEMS

Breathe in Four	19
This Morning	20
How We Think It Must Have Been	22
Sky and Soil	23
Vestment	24
In Praise of Drought	25
Letter to October	26
Portent	28
Fall Passover	29
Tortoise Shell	30
When the Boy Leaves the River	31
Why We Display the Broken	32
In the Church of January	34
Copperhead Dreams	36
Mountain Morning with Deer	38
Vespers	40
This, Her Art	42
On Finding My Father's Pocketknife in an Old Bag of Keys	43
Early Spring Prayer	44
The Ordinary	45

SELECTED POEMS
What the Night Told Me

Sentimental	51
Planting	52
Our Pact	54
On a Park Bench in Heaven	56
Eula's Quilt	58
Charit Creek	59
Telling the Bees	60
Talking to You Asleep	61
Night Song	62

The Art of Dying

Columbine 65
Strangers 66
Swimming Under Water 68
Value 70
Mounding Potatoes 72
Afternoon at Cades Cove 74
Otter Dream for Geron 76
From the Night Porch 78

Gods of Little Pleasures

Question and Answer 83
My Grandmother's Language 84
Buttons 86
Among Oaks 87
His Dust 88
Worship 90

Tatters

Tatters 93
My Brother's Hands, 1966 94
Damaged Child, Shack Town, Elm Grove, Oklahoma, 1936 . . . 95
The Names of Hats 96
First Snow 98
Deep-Running 100
Something I Can Name 102

Late Winter

Late Winter Longing 105
Lake Isle of Tennessee 106
And 107
The Body Washer, Iraq 2006 108
The Language of Rain 109
With the Help of Birds 110
Table Nine 112
Last Rite to the Queen of Grammar 114
Winter Wind Song 116
My Father Made Love 118
My Mother's Soul 120

The News Inside

The News Inside 123
The Melting 124
Dark Fire 125
Bookish 126
Listening to Japanese Music at Starbucks, I Think of Basho . . . 128
Myotis Lucifugus 130
Long Division 132
The Appointment 133
Wednesday Miracles 134
The Names of Creeks 136
Indigo 137
Journey 138

Elemental

The Way 141
The Light that Follows Rivers 142
The Bells 143
Elemental 144
Flying 146
Off Shore 147
Rare 148
Savor 150
Singularities 151
Rearview 152
Mauve 153
My Wife's Tattoo 154
Magic 155
Applesauce 156
Tortoise Morning 157
Start with a Bad Memory— 158
Something like Grace 160
Driving the County 162

Acknowledgments 165

About the Author 169

NEW POEMS

Breathe in Four

Cirrus clouds drift the sky eastward,
their movement so subtle, it takes a studied
gaze. The skeletal crowns of hardwoods
clue the eye, a mantra of sight and sound.

Years ago in Daddy's car, a blood moon
rose red above GrandMilt's farm, yellowed out
as moons must do. My heart seared bold
and thought about the stories my brothers told.

The rat terrier, Bob, killed rattlesnakes;
the Pritchard girl, beautiful and wild, found
drowned and naked in Beech River; her brother
hanged himself in the barn. Gothic whispers

of church women hanging laundry saw his ghost
hover over his sister's grave on Bible Hill.
Hard to tell what was real, or just secondhand,
coughed up in a john boat when fish weren't biting.

Today cirrus clouds drift eastward, shuffling
a pale February blue . The old man I've become
should let the stories die, flame with yard sticks
gathered for fire. My heart seeks winter mantras,

breathe in four, breathe out five, count starlings
as they make a winter tree a candelabra;
whisper a prayer for the beautiful and the wild,
as cirrus clouds map an eastern sky.

This Morning

...every glance at the world around you will be a sort of salvation.
        —William Stafford

Rain, night breeze,
    my home's green world—
oak, hickory, maple, gum
    umbrella the long porch
and its herb pots— mint, basil,
    rosemary, lemon sage.

I place a Gala apple on the table
    to honor Eve and the speckled
king snake climbing in the Rose
    of Sharon. How fortunate—
ancient symbols at peace
    in my garden. No damning,
no killing of Pascal lambs, no
    neighbor turned into salt
before her daughters. Not today.

This May morning, all are welcome,
    especially Jehovah's Witnesses
canvassing our county road
    with smiling pamphlets
in which Heaven resembles a summer
    picnic after church
except there are no gravestones
    to attach plastic flowers.

Mist rises from Sulfur Creek
    like incense, and I think how mother
loved the scent of plowed fields
    after rain, how one can almost hear
new seeds dreaming the verb *to be*.

Today I am a child learning to sing,
    a newt growing a new foot,
the sound of rain dripping through
    leaves.

How We Think It Must Have Been

Brother and sister once washed dishes
in front of a kitchen window and watched
cedar waxwings eat mulberries. Lilies lost

petals as evening lost itself among a gentle tedium
in a house of books, piano music and green beans.
A mother who sang off key waltzed with a father's

tenor which burst into song as natural as rain
when some 40's tune opened his mouth.
A new silence erupted into story—someone

ran away to get married, a hobo stopped
for a ham sandwich, a sick neighbor needed soup,
and the new preacher's sermon tasted as stale

as leftover potatoes. *Let's speak of roses*, father said.
Day closed with a girl reading a novel on her bed,
a boy at a window whispering to night as if it held
a gift dismissed as darkness. An attic fan pulled
fresh air through rooms and hummed a tune that
nurtured sleep: flesh, soft sheets and breathing,

as death snoozed in the oak with an owl,
and God sat on the porch steps, scratched
the spaniel's ears, and wished to be human.

Sky and Soil

    Fields dress with tan corn stubble
after harvest, crows take advantage

    of one row left to attract deer.
I think of my grandfather and brother,

    men of barns, horses and tilled land.
Not an easy life, but charmed in ways—

    something calls them to sky and soil,
pocket knives to trim finger nails,

    dogs in pickups, heads out windows
testing the air,

    prayers that go with nights awake
listening for thunder, the uncertain

    miracle of seed to fruit.
I can see them wake in the night

    to stroll wearing boxers,
holding themselves from fall chill.

    Harvest over, a full moon glows
behind a cloudbank then breaks

    free to shadow the earth with
tree and fence, making the old cemetery

    a harvest of sorts,
ghost-worthy with sorrow and praise.

Vestment

At first light we drove
past a country church
where the purple vestment
used to drape Christ's cross
had fallen around the ankle
of wood, far below
the holes in the palms,
the spear in the side.
I imagined hearing
soldiers gambling
for the robe and a jeer
of madness and grief
rising toward the sky
on a day that changed
the confused history
of our world. Yet,
a spring storm two
days after Easter
chose to belittle
the crucifixion,
or
maybe not—
an inch of rain
re-greened Spring.
Willows beside
Sulfur Creek dance
as a kingfisher rattles
her territorial song
above current ripples,
a crystal blue only April brings.
Sweet Jesus, my brother
whispers, fingering the air
outside his pickup window.

In Praise of Drought

Brown corn crinkles the color of work spots
on my father's hands. Wrens circle the porch
for seed, drink from metal pot I leave in the yard
like mother did. Drought-time, a place in her life
she couldn't leave in farm country, a place
that scalds the soul, brings memories of grandparents
and cousins in the fields casting fists of dust,
an omen sweet Jesus won't fix—six months
of labor flushed down the dung-hole.

Mother woke in the night, remembering porch whispers,
a drought child then, hearing language of failed crops,
whir of cicadas in late July, not words so much
as voice tones, and silence between talk.
Why ache helps children know family better,
how chosen words, looks away, reveal selves
that don't populate breakfast or Sunday dinners.
Praise be to moments true as dust and scorched earth,
heartbreak, powdered milk, Christmas singing,
and a stingy Santa Claus.

Father and Mother, now dust, their spirits
heavenward in their faith. Rain in late summer
brings hope back, brings men talking trash
beside pickups at the grocery store.
Their hearts tied to soil surrounding barns,
skies ever hopeful, ever endless.
What souls learn from hard-times—
smiles born in love, whispers in loss.
Parents' dreams of drought tight against me,
taught silence, mystery, who we really are,
who we must be.

Letter to October

The day is cool, windy,
and gray, clouds low—
morning proudly wakes
to rain. Sumac smiles
in the way plants smile,
moist leaves floating
and happy. Bark lichen,
an extra green, shares
its gallery of shapes,
never two alike. *Glory*,
my mother would say.
I can almost hear her
whisper from memory's
grave and its notion
of pretend. A few street lamps,
in their meticulous desire
to please, still think it's night.
When the sun burns through,
they go out, a little embarrassed—
everything's a measure, even hunger.
Not for food, really,
but an emotional manna,
how Fall's beginnings open
the heart to sorrow,
its shape, pulse-monitored.

Fall means so many things—
from grace, kicked out
of the garden, a broken leg
when no one spotted the ladder,
cries of a lost fledgling unable
to fly back to the nest. You
know the sound, the feeling
somewhere in the stomach pit.
Blue begins to outline clouds,
always needed. You can say
air molecules scattering light,
but I know it's the color
of my father's eyes.

Portent

We might have known
had we paid attention—
plants dying, Wandering Jew
and jade, basil and rosemary—
too much water, too little,
too much care, not enough—
omens that said this isn't her,
the one our tribe counted on,
who taught us how to prune
roses, weed gardens, dust
tomatoes; the one who urged
us to take our sorrow to trees,
to lake where it best served
the landscape or grassy minions
of steep hills, the journey
itself healing.   So we gather
away from windows where
she stood and take turns making
coffee, the kitchen a friend—
chipped dishes and maple table
patinaed with joy and heartache.
We wander to the far field
where she often went to smoke
her one cigarette, say her prayers
to an openness, rub the neighbor's
mare on the stripe above its nose.
You can kneel here better
than in a church—the sky an open eye,
earth, for better or worse, our home.

Fall Passover

Why in the great thoughtless sky
we seek solace…in the fickle wind's

thin soup we feel nourished…
in the plot-less story of October,

dusk hints resolution…
My mother, back from the grave,

speaks of heaven as if stardust,
our flesh and blood, is sacred,

and the crimson pokeberry juice
invading my yard might mark

the door lintel to keep the destroyer
at bay. After all, a Passover comes

when maples flush the yard red
and leaves carpet the deathless

minions of grass. Evening welcomes
a prayer meeting in which the call

and response of towhees sanctifies
the cooler air, and something like god

lights the evening star as surely
as she snuffs another out.

Tortoise Shell

An empty tortoise shell,
    its inhabitant once ambled

the forest behind my home—
    now a hollow floor and ceiling,

its ruin stripped clean by time
    and hunger, an orange

and black cottage, home
    to snails and small rodents

who wish to sit and watch
    loam's mystery.

It could be a sandal
    for a small savior,

one-legged Buddhist
    who hops among creation,

his vow of poverty proven
    by this humble hoof.

Or better yet, a miter
    for Saint Francis' head.

He sings his *Canticle of the Sun*—
    praise wind, rain, fire;

praise water, rock, shadow, light;
    praise spring, summer,

autumn, winter—
    journeys to our rightful night.

When the Boy Leaves the River

after Maggie Smith

When the boy leaves the river,
    the shadow of the heron
drifts through sycamores,
    their leaves an October flutter
coppered by cedar rust.
    How they sail on the water
like clouds the boy carries
    on his shoulders—the drift
of uncertainty, of journey.

When the boy leaves the river,
    the current remembers his sight,
how he sat on a rock and followed
    it through shoals and jumbled
birch-stuffed eddies, his eyes
    in concert with the sound of it,
how the osprey's shrill cry
    celebrates its kill.

In the city, traffic and light,
    and oil reflection in street-rain,
horns and tire swish—
    and a broken song,
a woman's sorrowed voice
    from a car window
fading with the distance—
    almost like a river barge
calling night away in sleep—
    and this is how he returns—
dreamscape in which loneliness feels
    kinship and the river flows.

Why We Display the Broken

> We make a dwelling in the evening air
> In which being there together is enough.
> —*Wallace Stevens*

Your grandmother's pie plate,
the wooden butter mold,
my father's shaving mug,
and unfinished painting
of a river in Vermont.

How the scatter of our daily
lives fractures our dreams:
phone calls of the newly stricken
alphabetized with last year's:
a fall, a head injury, an old woman's
sleeping pills that wouldn't help
her sleep forever, and cancer,
always cancer.

        And yet,
Jane Kenyon wrote *Let Evening Come*,
Stafford penned *Assurance*, and Stevens
would have lived one moment to watch
the brilliance of oil on water.

In the back yard a crippled crow
floats from a tree with an injured wing,
scavenges the seed under the feeder,
digs a grub from the woodpile, then
climbs the tree in hops and flutters
to safety. She survives each day,
but knows winter is a month away.

On the book shelf the cover of
an old poetry volume crumbles. I take it
down carefully and turn to marked
pages, reread and sample the notes
I scribbled four decades ago. Who
was that boy, I wonder, helping Frost
climb birches and harvest apples.

In the Church of January

Windows open
    a house
        to light snow,
 squirrels circling trees,
    woodpecker on roof.
        Her tapping, a drum solo,
sky, a halo
    above this little ridge
        on a small planet.
There lived a child once
    who accepted this day
        as a gift wrapped
in winter limbs
    cradling the sky.
        No busy-list to imprison,
morning an open gate
    on this side of tomorrow.
        Just listen to him hum
a tune his sister played
    on the piano,
        his daydream
a kitchen church—
    coffee brewing,
        scent of oatmeal and toast.

Decades later, a man
    hums the boy's tune,
        pours a cup,
his chest a cage—
    inside, forgotten footsteps
        on an oaken floor.
In his throat, a mumble,
    a small cough and years—
        memory excavates life's
vague museum site,
    weaves a silent prayer—
        each day growing
            three minutes
                of light.

Copperhead Dreams

Cedar glade, limestone crevasses
    ripe with copperheads.
My wife spies a rust pattern.
    We just make out its viper head,
diamond shaped, an arrow
    aimed at nothing.
So still it lies, stuffed
    with its warm-blooded prey
to survive the winter.
    Tissue will chill, heart beat
a mumble as the body's
    engine idles the slow burning.
Does the snake's sleep dream
    fatted mice, fox squirrels,
or is this darkness as cold as death,
    a practice for the longest night?

A tunnel wrought in human dreams
    funnels a cave,
a design measured
    centuries in the blood.
Imagine months of anxious sleep,
    dreams awaken, briefcase lost,
cell dead, dial stuck
    on your mother's deathbed,
her empty mouth a dark closet
    you can't escape,
your lost child unsaved, just out of reach.

But then there's the thaw,
    a bear sow emerges from her den
with two cubs to graze on sedge,
    and a copperhead
with shiny new scales,
    ornery and piqued,
hunts with heat sensors
    for warm blood.

Mountain Morning with Deer

Dawn, woven by birch limbs,
dances in the loom of a low-cloud sky.

Barely breathe, you whisper,
as one hand widens the tent flap,

and the other, a numb codger,
fingers the air to wake the day.

Deer grazing Roan Bald,
barley visible, seem to float

above swaying broomsage.
Sun up with no sun, a thrall of time

we can't undo, even if we wish
and we don't. Nothing defiant

about a mountain scored with quiet,
and the drift of tall grass in wind.

So we settle in, canteen water,
saltines and cheese, a dollop

of peanut butter, our journals
marked with laurel leaves.

I write of almost stepping on
a junco nest filled with eggs.

You describe chestnut-sided
warblers in rhododendron.

We both write of towhees
singing night to bed.

You note something's going
to happen, I note something did.

Vespers

The sun leaves the sky
like the sky leaves the lake,
light searching ripples, as if
wishing to stay—My neighbor
carries a sack of vegetables
from the garden saying, *time to wash up*,
as if his clock is set by the planet.
My grandfather did the same,
scrub with a cake of soap
at the kitchen sink so he smelled
the steam from cooking.
                              Today
something in me needs simple words—
ways and habits scheduled by life
beyond the six o'clock news—
the way we held hands at the maple table
to bless soup beans, cornbread,
and a slice of onion—more family
than religion, an earth reverence,
childhood charmed by rivers,
and hilltop ponds. Spit from the bridge
and watch a fish rise in Cub Creek.

                         On the Ridge
a thrush ushers in the evening
with a little mate song. I pause,
sit on porch steps and listen to a train
woo a new moon. I climb the ladder
of places I've lived, sixty-four years
of tucking the sun in bed. I think
about how night settles differently
in each location, notice my wife behind me
and rest my head against her knees,
admire how moonlight drapes
its silver shawl around her shoulders.

This, Her Art

What you heard wasn't the towhee grubbing
forest loam, wasn't tiny claws digging
for seeds, but Suzanne's fingers placing

birch bark and shell shards on textured
canvas. It's not your fault, her hands are
bird-like, as are her green eyes, the way

they search the sky for rain, for bunting,
and the raucous affection of crows.
Don't let the sounds fool you—her art

is porcupine quills, twist of vine around
a beech twig, wooden beads polished
and stitched on handmade paper.

The sigh you hear could be wind in pine
as she steps back to study the becoming,
an iris blossom almost in bloom.

The tapping isn't a sapsucker pecking
for larvae, no, it is her heartbeat as she touches
her design, her blood so near the source.

On Finding My Father's Pocketknife in an Old Bag of Keys

A grandmother's hands peeling apples,
frying eggs, a tiny kitchen, white goat

and barbwire compliment a dream
with pasture pond, willow-lined,

leaves fingering wind. Puzzle pieces
never fit except in tightening ribs.

Gourd dipper hanging above a spring,
a locust fencepost flashed with tin,

brass candlesticks covered in melt.
A boy picked wax beads and smoothed

them between fingers and thumb.
October's chill finds a flannel shirt,

splotched heavy with wood smoke
and old man sweat. Perfect for windfalls

ready to burn. It's what won't burn
I pull from silence, hold in my skin.

Early Spring Prayer

It's easy to worship something you can't see—
it doesn't melt, can't be covered by snow,
or burn or rot—it doesn't seem to care about

the physics of the visual. It doesn't have
a shadow that shrinks as it ages. And best
of all, it makes of us temporary gods,

requests that we feed the poor, heal
the sick, battle evil, right injustice.
At the end of March, black gum

and maple bud, crocuses and daffodils
abound, now snow-dusted. And today,
I spied a cerulean warbler at Sulfur Fork.

When it flew the blue stopped my breath.
The invisible listens so well, unlike humans
who plan a response while you talk. Oh,

invisible one, be with me until my shadow
dissipates, teach me to seek beauty in the visual,
to even love all that too soon disappears.

The Ordinary

Outside my study window, March
tries to prepare itself for spring.
A shagbark hickory, draped in vines,
seems scant in its winter drab—a cardinal

awaiting its turn at the feeder, a lost rose
among the tangle. A cooper's hawk,
in his copper camouflage, swoops
into the broom sage, its talons forward.

The day carries on without my help,
tends to its business. From my perch
I'm just an odd fellow in an ordered world.
There is something numinous in the ordinary,

light and shadow, decay— not *go to heaven*
holy, but infinite just the same—
the leaf mold organisms in my patch
of forest outnumber humans on our planet.

At the cusp of memory the present
sits, waiting for the world to make sense.
So I'll get another cup of coffee,
heat up leftover soup, do something

useful, change the cat litter,
join the movement. The sun burns
haze from morning clouds, bones
in the Methodist Cemetery stretch

a little to hear a train warn cars at
the crossroad, and the cooper's hawk,
clutching a furry knot, calls shrill and
clear as it wings its prey toward home.

SELECTED POEMS

What the Night Told Me

Sentimental

I used to wake clouded to a window
mother had just opened. The billow
of curtains shadowed my bed,
and my blood's cadence mingled
with hammering in neighborhood garages.
My bones would spring when deaf old Martha
swept her walk with the teeth of a rake,
and goose bumps roamed my shoulders
like leaves crossing roof gutters.

I flattened both feet on the hardwood floor,
smelled toast burning in the stove, and heard
mother's forgetful hum drift from the clothesline.

This is how I think it must have been
when I wake to the scent of burning leaves,
my dream scatters shadows across the yard.
Then I remember her soft hum
above the fond flap of sheets,
and my cares wave as empty
as shirt sleeves in the morning sun.

Planting

The first four years
I slept in the whispering
landscape of my parents' room.
My cot was cornered under
the breeze-way window
of that frame farm house.
At first dark, my close friends
were the tic-tock tail
of a righteous lab
and Pocahontas, the calico cat,
perched on his back
like a scout.

During cool nights when
my mother's skin shone
velvet beneath her soft gown,
I learned my first private words:
Is he asleep?
Was that the dog?
And when I was very quiet,
my parents wrestled their land,
cleared stones with hot palms,
broke clods with strong hips,
and spread breathless across that bed,
a harmony of shoulders and knees.

Most nights this curiosity was lost
to the yearning of tree frogs,
the passion of owls through
the soft dance of muslin
in the breeze.
I learned the safe tunnel
of childhood sleep,
as innocent as any given night,
sweeter than the smell
of spring planting.

Our Pact

My brother would read my quiet sorrow,
follow me to our room and stand
at the door staring while I sulked
on the bed, head toward the wall.
When I turned to confront him, I'd catch
dirty shorts in my face. "Lighten up,"
he'd say, "you ain't dead yet."

I'd perform my leaping tackle
and he'd tickle me until I gave up,
half silly and drunk with anger.
We'd laugh at my teenage grief,
how goddamn serious I was
about football and Becky Lewis.
She dumped me once a week.

At night he'd fart under the covers,
claim it was an earthquake, and the bed
shook like a life boat in a storm.
Camping at Price's Pond, he found
a black flint arrowhead which he would
rub before calling a host of owls around
our fire loud enough to wake the dead.

These frames passed through my head
like coming attractions at the picture show
this morning as I woke to the pastel light
of hospital green. My brother's vital signs
blipped across the screen and his lips
quivered for the words an aneurysm
had stolen from his tongue.

I found myself saying, "Lighten up,
you ain't dead yet, you ain't
dead yet," saying it over and over
until the phrase became our secret pact,
as powerful as black arrowheads,
magic owl calls, and his tight grip
on my hand.

On a Park Bench in Heaven

On a park bench in heaven,
my grandparents sit staring
through all that holiness
which glimmers, they think,
like freezing rain on winter trees.

They were pleased to be here
at first, flattered to be taken
despite all their Sunday plowing.
The pearly gates are just fine,
my grandmother says, but she
would trade the lot for a tin of snuff.

My grandfather would sell
his soul for a pocket watch;
he's tired of asking every saint
that flies by what time it is.

All this gold and silver remind them
of the dining room at the Holiday Inn.
What they really miss is the smell
of honeysuckle or the way
woodland violets circle star trillium
like a wedding quilt in spring.

We've been here twenty years,
my grandfather says,
and to date, no funerals,
no sick friends, no floods,
no droughts, no nips of sour mash
at the general store
on Saturday afternoons.

And harp music day and night,
not one angel flat-picks
or sings a whiskey tenor.
In the pickup glove compartment
of his heart, he wonders if hell
wasn't more like Tennessee.

Eula's Quilt

After three on summer afternoons,
bright pastures rise beyond fence and brook
to the dark green of Braintree Mountain
high against the Vermont sky.
Last winter's snow inspired me
to work a quilt giving back
summer's ridge and pasture.

So it was in this June landscape
from my kitchen window that three gliders
like hawks flew their way up from Marsh's Run
trailing huge shadows across the meadow.
I watched with envy, longing to swap places
to see how accurate a rendering my quilt
had been. Two disappeared over the top.
The third circled back, edged the pasture
and skimmed the ridge again. The phone
call from Lewis told the story.

A glider had crashed in the deep ravine
behind the Oliver place. A New Hampshire man
had died from severe head injuries. My grandson
asked me why a man would risk his life so.
I said, *Son, at 83 I risked my life last winter
checking the mail.* All fooling aside,
at my age, I mourn the loss of risk.
Every time I pull out this quilt to see pastures
leading toward the mountain where maple
gives way to fir, I see a glider's shadow crossing
spring green and sage brown, getting larger and
larger before it folds into the darkest quilt panel.

Charit Creek

Charity, you had crossed the wide beech log
a hundred times to visit Station Hollow.
When you didn't return by late afternoon,
your father took cedar knots from the shed,
lit a lantern, and traced the path
to branch creek crossing.
In an eddy a hundred yards down,
he witnessed the light flicker on your
long brown hair as it swirled
in the current like river kelp.
You hung U-shaped, caught at the waist
on a birch log: one white arm flapped
as if it meant to touch your toes.
He told Jake Hatfield that he couldn't
pull you out himself; the night held
the memory of your hazel eyes, the slight
blush of cheek, the thin lips which parted
when you smiled.

Over a hundred years later,
an old man mentions this to me,
how Charit Creek got its name.
I sit on a boulder to conjure your story
from this winter day. High above,
buzzards circle stone bluffs. Sycamore bones
reflect from water. They wind and flap
as the wind shutters the surface.
These stark arms make the snow whiter,
and I think of you, dear Charity,
the awful look on your face
as the limbs reach out against the sky
wearing starlings like clothes pins.

Telling the Bees

(Mountain legend says when a death occurs,
a member of the family is sent to tell the bees,
or harm will come.)

That week Luke Hughes was found
two days gone with his throat torn.
GrandSally saw the new moon
through a window pane and the bees
came in my dream. Thousands spread
like a giant carpet flying Luke
away to Jesus. I woke with a start,
dressed and left the house, ordained.
Up Cub Creek I stopped to drink,
dipped the tin cup and saw my neck
distort with pain. Nobody knew
what tore Luke's throat.
Around each laurel corner I paused
to listen, and imagined every space
as a man's shape marked by root and stone.
On the high meadow the bee boxes
greeted me like temples carved white
against the blue-green grass.
I turned each to the right three times
and stood before them proclaiming
Lukas G. Hughes is dead by the power
of a new moon, and Sally Brown sent
me here to let you know.
The bee buzz grew round me,
and the blood of Luke Hughes
was harvested and turned to wax.

Talking to You Asleep

Searching the drawer for matching socks,
I watched you sleeping and
it dawned on me how much
I like cutting tall weeds in the orchard
while you mow the grass.
The orchard's five rows
of shadows move
in strange regiment
through the day.
Listen, we have fought
twenty years successfully,
sometimes for, sometimes
against, often times
just for the sake of fighting,
and I still smile when
you get up in the dark
and trip over my hiking boots.
When you crawl over me
to get on your side of the bed,
you pay me back
with your sharp knees.
We have five degrees, two cats,
and an old farm house.
In this morning quiet
your hair still falls in barmaid tangles
against your pillow.
The only movement is through
the window by your head,
wind breaking orchard shadows
when leaves dapple them with light.

Night Song

for Robert

All night trees rained
leaves against the roof.
Hickory, maple, and oak
palmed and scraped
wood and tin, combed
the air like ghost hands
freed from the arms of men
who grieved with hands.

And in the illogic of half sleep
the side of my brain which understands
my heart heard the song of the leaves
as they tossed across the night.

I have lived among these trees for years,
and we have felt the sky's weight
heavy on our seed. We are passengers
on this gracious rock which circles
a dying star.

And some nights I take this on faith,
that the same glue which holds
my life in balance, allows
the earth to fly the moon
like a kite and scatters these leaves
through this night, homeward.

The Art of Dying

Columbine

(Middle English from Medieval Latin,
meaning dove-like, comparing the inverted
flower to a cluster of five doves.)

The roar of the Little River
as it rushes towards Cades Cove
makes intermittent conversation a shout.
We point and smile, mind reading
as we course the steep bank of the stream.
You wait behind a house-size rock,
grab my elbow, and pull me to a stone wall
where you have found the columbine.
A hundred blossoms grow against dark slate,
purple, orchid pink and spidery. The flowers nod
their heads as the river breeze circles the canyon.
You pinch one and invert it in your palm
so I can see the five dove silhouettes clustered
by veined beautiful flesh. And I have to think,
how like your wild hair these columbine
grow, delicate and spindly.
You climb out on a ledge and cast
this blossom into the furious spray.
A trout rises slightly before the flower
is swept through a long cascade.
I imagine it torn in the current,
freeing the five doves which spread
wings and lift from the surface
to fly into the mountains.
I glance back at the muted colors
and then to the bright blue of the spring sky.
I say the word *columbine* slowly,
careful to mouth the three syllables:
col um bine, col um bine, how lovely.
I turn to follow, keeping my distance
from your discoveries
as we go this way.

Strangers

Seventeen split my tongue
like a pet crow's, shrill,
mimicking, irreverent,
ignorant, and shamed.

My glances were foul
balls, my hopes were
shooting stars, I was
batting zero.

I ate spaghetti
with a pitchfork, picked my teeth
with an ax, wrecked more cars
than a test dummy.

I measured out love
with tweezers, was as humble
as a chainsaw, and when my sincerity
was challenged,

cracked open my heart
like a coconut, the pure
sweet insides for all
to taste and marvel.

My hands were foxes,
my thoughts shot blanks,
my smile was as sweet
as plastic grapes.

My dreams were strangers
who stood on a dark bridge
hiding their eyes from
the sun.

I was angry at my dead
father, I was hunting
Jesus on the cover
of record albums.

And one of the strangers
on the bridge? It was just
me three years older, tongue
sewed together,

mouth clamped shut,
army-mummed, staring down
on seventeen, wondering where
the hell I'd come from.

Swimming Under Water

for Andy

My nephew and I swim in Kentucky Lake.
He swirls under the surface
and pops up ten feet away
as I breast-stroke slowly toward open water.
His eyes sparkle as he tells me
about his mile-swim at camp.

I see his dead mother as a child,
a quiet freshness both complex and shy.
This sense of her swells from his voice
and face as I kick at a sudden grief
which starts in the chilled water
around my feet and rises through
the hollow of my own death
until I turn and swim away.

Can a child completely heal
from a mother killed by fire?
Beverly forced herself back
into the burning house.
I can still see the closed coffin,
hear my brother's twisted laughter.
Grief shook him like an empty shirt in a storm.

Andy says he swims best under water,
eyes closed tight, his limbs pushing
the darkness behind him like the past.
I dunk his head and dive in a game of tag,
and, pulling hard to get away,
I realize that Kentucky Lake holds
enough water to douse every house fire
in America, that it is filled with evaporated
tears of centuries of children, that with
its depth and length, my nephew could
swim with his eyes closed forever.

Value

for Tony

Walking the hill
I quit mowing years ago,
I spy a doe and her fawn
before she smells me. I crouch
on a log to watch as they
amble quietly, chewing sawbriar
and eating green shoots
rain has brought back
from summer drought.

The flanks of the fawn
still wear spots dappled
like light through orchard
leaves on the barn.
The small birth feathers
cling to her maturing hide
and catch between twigs
of sassafras and devil sticks.

When they pass onto
the ridge behind the junipers,
I creep forth to collect
fawn wool captured
by brush. Oh, I am
quite sure it is good
for nothing, and yet good
for everything, coarse hair rubbing
between forefinger and thumb.

A hand full of fawn spots,
like an ancient fetish,
wards off the world's
measure of value.
I cling to it tight and think
about those innocent sure steps,
a grace I have only mastered in dreams
when the heaviness of being human
escapes Newton's law
and lets me drift, sailing fawn hair
into late afternoon.

Mounding Potatoes

The phone call at 2 a.m.
was my sister saying
that you had died in
the emergency room
but had been shocked
to life so that your pulse
stabilized, and you told
the doctor you remembered
the whole event, heart stopping
and the sharp electric trip back.

He said that such a memory wasn't likely.
But you stuck to your story
even during the ambulance ride
to the medical center where
magical balloons sailed
their timely voyage through your blood
to stretch the vessels
which clogged your heart.

Mother, today you smile at my concern,
knowing what death is like.
At eighty-two, you heard
no voices from beyond,
no angelic music fluttering
a heavenly welcome.
Your faith was stuck
in the strength of this world
as the frantic voiced commands
and the laying on of fire
kept you in life's routine.

Two weeks later, I marvel to watch
your strong hands mound
young plants in my garden,
dreaming the while
of new potatoes with parsley,
resurrected from
this simple ground.

Afternoon at Cades Cove

Along the edge of woods
deer crept past us
like the afternoon
toward the ridge barn
where we later hid,
our heads pressed together
behind a board crack
to spy the silent herd
moving between
shadows of trees
like light flickering
with leaves,
and suddenly an old doe
sensed us hidden close,
raised her head toward the woods,
coughed three shrill barks,
and the afternoon almost stopped
that such a startled sound
could burst from grace.

We escaped
the darkness of the barn
and rock-hopped down a sparkling brook
racing toward the road,
and in an eddy beneath
dogwood buds, we found
a clutch of bones
crowned with a buck skull.
Its hollow eyes
scorched our flesh
as they gazed through us,
past the barn
where we had hidden,
past the wooded ridge
where deer had streamed,
past the slight touch
of spring nestled
in the dark limbs
with the sun.

Otter Dream for Geron

Jogging by the New River,
I noticed the winter stream's
blue-green depth between white shoals.
Suddenly like a submerged bobber
the sleek head of otter
popped up and with his skilled body
swirled against a sycamore root
and lay on his back to eat a mussel.

Brother, I thought of you in another time zone,
under the glare of an operating light,
gloved and masked, pinning
a fractured leg so that a child might walk.
I know about your harried life—
you rush from clinic to hospital to home.
You try to heal the sick and raise
grown children who will not stay grown.

I would have you like the otter,
who, in his struggle to eat,
takes time to play. I would have
your life healed with this river,
nurtured by the soft fur of the otter's belly,
the joy of jogging by such freedom,
these shoals which roar a line of spray
one hundred yards across.

Thinking these thoughts for you,
I imagine that we wade into the stream together,
and spying the feeding lips of trout,
cast our flies and watch fish pop the bait,
fling from the water like crone
sculptures against the sky.
I am not blind to the fact
that caring for others heals you.

Today my wish is that
a river seep into your dreams
to bring you joy.

From the Night Porch

The silhouette of Snow Ridge,
trees tossing in wind-shears
from a coming storm,
reminds me of a flight

from L.A. home to
Tennessee: the jerking plane,
the bolts of lightning
by the wing. A woman

asked to close my shade
as if fear of crashing
would be lessened by
what she could not see.

Her voice was like my
sister's, soft and straight,
who once told me when
I was small and scared:

"Darkness is your friend,
a twin to match the cave
you have inside."
Listen:

Memory is easily broken
by the sound of trees,
the sound of trees
erased by memory.

The dark ridge above
the creek is rich
with both.
A flash of lightning,

I count
one Mississippi
two Mississippi, three—
then thunder:

storms are like the future,
three miles away,
closing fast.
The cave I have inside

is opened by the wind,
like the dark ridge
surprised by lightning
and the rush of leaves.

Many times I stand
on this porch
to watch storms fill up
with trees,

and hear my sister's voice
in the night
speak of darkness
as a friend.

This memory
without fear
webs me to the night
beauty of this land.

Gods of Little Pleasures

Question and Answer

Would it matter if after supper
the snow sifting against the window
visited your dreams, each flake
in slow motion, counting down
the winters since your father's death?

Of course, it won't happen until,
looking in a mirror,
you notice hair growing
from your ear like his.
And that shadow, the one

passing over your heart
like a cloud drifting across
the sun, consider it a sign
of maturity, that you've
earned the right to hope.

Look on the bright side
until it blinds you: the snow
doesn't care about your dreams.
It blankets your father's grave
to keep him warm.

Consider the shadow across
your heart as shade, the coolness
beneath the maple beside your
childhood home. Go there,
the old dog is waiting.

My Grandmother's Language

In my grandmother's language
there was no word for sex.
Cows were playful in season,
too many bucks on the road,
quail paired off in spring,
she's ripe as a plum,
don't do nothing foolish.

She never said work, but some things
needed tending, the ox was in the ditch,
it's going to rain tomorrow,
make hay, put food on the table.
Idle hands, my grandmother scolded.
Nobody got tired either, but plumb tuckered,
asleep in his supper, stiff-jointed, plow-weary.

A skunk was a polecat, a pig was a shoat,
snakes were adders, and a panther was a painter.
No one ever heard of a metal detector
with some middle-aged retiree
searching beneath local baseball
bleachers for pocket change.
But there was real buried treasure,
Confederate gold on Johnson Hill,
family silver in McDonalds' orchard,
and soil, if treated right, rich enough to yield.

There was no voodoo, but haints were
bad spirits, and good ghosts hovered
over the Primitive Baptist cemetery,
billowing lights which were omens.

And in the undertow of sleep,
fingers were lost breaking sod,
skulls cracked by stubborn mules,
hands crushed by the crank of chains,
arms nubbed at the sawmill, and children
drowned, snake bit, or lured into
Dark Hollow alone.

In my grandmother's language there was
no word for handout, but people practiced
common decency. Neighbors were welcome
to share a table, no matter how sparse
the larder. Guests ate first and, during hard luck,
community stock shared community feed.
The words help and hope were the same.
"Can I hope you?" Grandmother asked,
of friends and strangers alike.

Buttons

In my mother's sewing drawer
we found a bag of buttons:
cloth-covered, brass, glass,
plastic, wooden, mother-of-pearl;
buttons small enough for a man's
shirt collar, large enough for car coats,
rain slickers, 40's woolen skirts;
buttons shaped like stars, flowers,
clover, bows, pumpkins, footballs,
and in the bottom, a pewter crucifix,
the needle holes in Christ's hands.

I could see my mother threading
the needle, doubling stitches, tying
her special knot in the material backing.
No one within my mother's view
went without buttons. In high school,
my friends tucked in their shirts
to keep her at bay. "Stop," she
would say, "something's missing
on your collar."

My sister and I clean her closets
of her clothes. Coats and dresses, some
fifty years old, are neatly buttoned
in place. We pack them for Goodwill,
then sit at the kitchen table over coffee.
We divide the buttons, fight for
the best ones, shamelessly bargaining
over the pewter crucifix, as Roman
soldiers did Christ's robe.

Among Oaks

July heat radiates ghosts
from the stones in the graveyard.
Graying tobacco barns stare
at the scorched blades of corn.
My grandmother, at forty, sits
in the shade of post oaks
snapping beans with her neighbors.
Leaf whispers in the hot wind
soften talk mummed by drought.

My mother, at forty, holds
my infant sister. She drifts
in a wicker swing with oak shadows
brushing the porch. Late summer heat
can't douse her pleasure that my father
has come home from the war.
A new child, unplanned, grows inside her.
Something she can't name aches for fall.

Still curved like a girl, my wife,
at forty, stands on porch steps.
A June breeze burns the tip
of her cigarette like incense.
Her worries reach like a troubled child
toward her mother's aged cares.
Oak limbs hide the yard from a sere sky.
Fireflies rise from parched grass like
the prayers of sisters far from home.

His Dust

for GrandMilt

Dust is my grandfather's business,
dust on sumac and cedar,
dust on dust as it flares
behind his tractor.

Dust loves my grandfather,
follows him around the farm,
creeps along the age lines
in his forehead, darkens
the crow's feet around his eyes,
cracks like creek mud
when he smiles.

When rain comes,
it meshes in his fields,
cradles his seeds until
the dance unfolds them
in straight rows.

I have seen him sift soil
through his fingers
in the morning breeze
or cast it above his head
before a storm.

I have seen him read
dirt in his cupped hands
like a psalm. For fifty
years it has been his
matins and his vespers,
hymns of hard work
and sacrifice.

January soil knows the scruff
of my grandfather's boots.
While other farmers are
caged inside, he walks
the soil he cannot work,
head straight, eyes combing
the contour of our farm.
There is no sadness like
my grandfather's winter whistle.
His lips purse, composing
green into the soil.

In the barn his tools lie
sharpened and clean,
his motors tuned.
In the field his hands
grope his pockets,
clutching fists of dust
he won't let go 'til spring.

Worship

I open the wood stove
and hear something escape the chimney.
Maybe the ghost of last May,
a month too warm for burning,
when we built a roaring fire
and left the doors open.
There's a spirit in a stove.
When I was twenty, I scoffed
at myths like the hearth god.
At fifty I'll practice any ritual
born from simple human need,
god of morning coffee and Sunday papers;
god of lazy love-making, wine, and old books;
god of tilling, planting, and harvesting.
I won't recognize the god of television,
videos, or cellular phones,
but the god of tractors,
handmade tools, raking leaves,
and sweeping the porch.
Praise be to the god of sheets billowing
like sails in the sun and the dank god
of storm cellars, spidery and safe.
I kneel willingly to the god
of stirring soup and kneading bread,
to all gods of needful work.
So this morning after hearing
the stove god haunt the chimney,
I kindle the first fall fire
to all the gods of necessity
who keep us fed and warm,
and to the gods of little pleasures
who help us to be kind.

Tatters

Tatters

From the bluff above Tim's Ford,
a brace of wood ducks squeal across
the lake into the wooded hollow.
Even in late winter some birds
pair off for spring, and it being
evening, find their roost.
You, my wife, my friend, my lover,
are holed up in this cabin
surrounded by beech and hickory
where the tatters of old leaves
still cling to limbs. The roadside
bombs in Baghdad, the commuter
massacre in Spain, and the bodies
of children found shot and stacked
in a house in California are tatters too
that cling to our visual memories,
though the TV is unplugged
and we have no newspapers.
Much has been said about the toll
images take upon the mind and body,
how much thankful guilt the fortunate
endure; though we pour a glass of wine,
eat fresh trout caught below the dam,
watch rain pock the surface of the lake
as night consumes cedars' hooded shadows
and the last gulls wing their way toward shelter.

My Brother's Hands, 1966

My oldest brother home from med school,
our family took iced tea into the backyard
beside the wet weather creek to enjoy
the oak broken sun of Sunday. To my joy
and my mother's jitters, my brother
lifted a rat snake that crawled
up to rest its head on his shoe.
With the gentle precision of his hands
that would one day be a surgeon's,
he let my sister and me touch its skin
as the snake roped between his fingers.

What I never told came late that afternoon.
I crept back by the stream to find the snake,
but boys from the Baptist picnic found it first,
and steeped in their parents' lore,
stoned it into oblivion. With sticks,
so as not to touch it, they hung the snake
on the Hansons' fence, perhaps
to ward off evil or bring rain
to the desert in their hearts.

Within a year my brother's hands
bandaged soldiers in Viet Nam,
as my mother wrung her hands in prayer,
and mine were busy banging out
protest songs on a Sears' guitar.
At night I dreamed the physician's hands
holding a serpentine staff instead
of a crucifix, blessing the foreheads
of boys he couldn't save.

Damaged Child, Shack Town, Elm Grove, Oklahoma, 1936

from a photo by Dorothea Lange

You stand against the muted grays of aged tin and stone.
Barn shadows almost hide bruised cheeks and arms.
A handsome quality frames your face, heavily browed eyes

narrowed into a thin defiant gaze: a look that says
you'll bust someone's balls if they're not careful. It's hard
to say if the shirt you wear, with one strap tied in a knot

on your right shoulder, was once a man's sleeveless,
or from a woman's cotton shift. I've seen children
with your stare, who know more than their years suppose.

They have stood in containment camps from Palestine
to Rwanda, and on city streets from Memphis to Los Angeles.
I won't make stories of how your mother clutched you

to her breast to shield you from your father's drunken breath,
nor imagine tender moments when your grandpa taught you
how to fish, nor shiver at what night's darkness brought.

You wear the slight grin of the proud and hungry,
too smart not to know a rotten world when you've
found one, and, cruelly, too smart not to dream.

The Names of Hats

An aigrette is a hat decorated
with egret tail feathers. Looking up
a word in the dictionary, I saw
a picture of a French woman
wearing one. I thought of the egret roost
outside of my home town.
It was a glorious sight, hundreds
of white birds gathered in trees
at the edge of a swamp,
carrying on mating rituals.
Of course, a housing development,
with a name like Quail Ridge,
was built close by. The swamp
was drained, the egrets killed
or driven off to stop histoplasmosis.
Twenty years ago, I taught school
with a man who had the malady.
He contracted the disease
on a Saturday outing
when he entered a boarded up
train station filled with pigeons.
He was a bitter little man
who chain smoked and complained
of ignorant students who wouldn't read.
He sued the train company
and waited years to win
enough money to stop teaching.
It never happened. Last May,
my wife and I went fishing
at Reelfoot Lake. It was a day
filled with the surprise of egrets.

In territorial feeding disputes,
they chased each other from lily pads
to snake grass to cypress roots,
squawking, flashing snow white wings,
and flaunting curved heron necks.
I don't know how most hats
get their names, or, if human fates
and birds' were reversed, whether egrets wouldn't
adorn their hats with my wife's golden hair,
just that on page 27 of my dictionary,
the word, aigrette, started memories
that led to stories that led me here.

First Snow

The snow clouds make a negative
of winter trees, except for the wind's
slight shaking and the twirl of leaves,
brown and crinkled on a distant branch.
She watches the hawk's low spiral
and knows that juncos have fluffed
breast feathers against the cold.
Some mornings sorrow is kept
at bay by detail. Yesterday's sun
shone bright, and she sat on the porch
to warm her face. A large doe stormed
the yard, stopped to look at her,
then sprinted the drive to the road.
Last night she dreamed it again
before a noise startled her from sleep.
She checked the door and heated milk
to drink. "Move in with us," her daughter
kept saying, "I wouldn't live alone
so far from town in that creaking house."
"You were born in this creaking house,"
she thought to say, but didn't. She's lost
the need to explain. Some nights regret
sets the dinner table and windows reflect
places she hasn't seen—her husband's grave,
the child who died at birth, the girlish
blush when old dreams wake a fever.

She's gained a faith that has little to do
with town preaching or her daughter's
misled concerns. A coyote raised
a brood below the barn last spring,
and she kept it secret. Pups tumbled
in the grass to draw their mother in a fray.
As snow begins to fall, she prepares a cage
of suet for mockingbirds. Tired bones
and sleepless nights come with the package.
A person learns to love a place or hate it.

Deep-Running

She knows that summer
creeps at evening tide:
sloughs receive their herons,
sassafras and willow
frame open water, cypress
stand knee deep in duckweed,
and raccoons seine shallows
for crayfish.

In her heart a cricket sings,
but in her head the hum
of neon wakes her. Light,
always outside her room,
frames the crack beneath
the door, monitors foot traffic,
mop and broom.

She turns on her side
and whispers, *deep-running*,
her father's word for the river
beyond the levee; and then
behooved, the measure
of her mother's code.

She presses her lips tight
to say *pipsissewa*, Cherokee
herb that stays green all winter,
and *persimmon*, smell of sweet
musk on the forest edge in fall.

She mouths these words
when sleep hides until she drifts
like mist on pools where
screech owls conjure ghosts,
and her father stands on a berm,
a night heron, lifting his arms
like wings.

Something I Can Name

At my kitchen table, I am
rushing toward something
unexpected like the scent
of dried dianthus my wife pressed
in a book, like the shape of a wren
fledging from a gourd, like a gold finch
eating thistle from a stem, like
the tail of a dead fox flaming
from the road in the wind.

I am rushing toward some seismic
rumbling in my skull, some volcanic
eruption in my heart, some longing
nestled in the bones of my feet.
I find my hands around a cup
of coffee gone cold. I take a sip
and choke on some opaque
desire to shake off my skin like
a dog emerging from a lake.

What time is it? It is time
for my blood to carry oxygen
to my cells, for a transference of faith
through something like osmosis
into the stardust in my bones,
in my cartilage, in my hair, in my nails.
It is time for the fault of disbelief to crumble,
time for some terrible angel to take me
like a rattle, shake me from the manners
of malls and mediocrity, from the concrete
and steel of convention centers, from
the magnifying glass of science, shake me
from the world that I can name.

Late Winter

Late Winter Longing

Lapping lake water reminds me of homesick Yeats.
A crow barks a string of caws from a sycamore snag,

and in the background, a barn owl haunts the afternoon.
I am homesick for all the homes I ever lived in,

the morning and evening light that shaped our longing,
for the dead who go on dying, and the living who wait to die.

Out the window, rows of waves blaze in the sun, and though
this is not my home, just a lakeside inn, I am homesick

for the ridge rising beyond the shore, how little cedars poke
through winter trees. Another month and a shimmer of green

will brush the ridge, and a different homesickness will form
like willow leaves, reminding me of how my mother said willow

with a certain lilt, as if to catch its dance in the fleeting breeze.

Lake Isle of Tennessee

Power points run the university.
Bullets space-out data on the screens, students
at laptops finger notes. I drop the bottled water
that I found in the faculty lounge and recall a tin cup

and GrandMilt's spring. It burbled from a nook beneath
a cottonwood and formed the head waters of Cub Creek.
Like homesick Yeats, *I will arise and go now* down
Interstate 40, to the Parson's exit, cut the back roads

to Bible Hill where my grandparents are buried
in the Baptist Cemetery, and try to find the spring
behind the convenience store that replaced
my father's birth house. My sister and I played

in the dog trot, wary of the rooster who ruled the yard.
When GrandMilt had finished chores and eaten breakfast,
he saddled Nell and cantered us to the spring where
spotted newts cleaned the water as it bubbled

from beneath the ground. Wipe the tin cup with a cloth,
he'd say, jiggle a little water to wash away the dust,
be careful not to muddle, lean from the spring
and drink, he whispered, and we did.

And

Friday, home from work, I flip on the war
and watch a group of marines help a family

bury their dead, and it seems that soldiers
called the car to stop with bull horns, but

was the driver deaf? No one knew, so the car
was destroyed, and the Shia women

wail and wave their hands against losing
what they love, against the charred remains,

and the marines stare at their feet,
and one young man being interviewed can't

look at the camera, and the Imam proclaims
them martyrs, says that they are already

with God, and the sand and dirt pitch
from the shovels as holes deepen,

and the desert sun cannot prevent
the holes from filling up with shadows,

and the deeper, the darker they become
until the bodies are lowered and

the wailing and waving of hands
continue and one of the town fathers

let's the translator kiss him
on the customary cheek.

The Body Washer, Iraq 2006

after hearing an interview on NPR

The body washer remembers her first corpse,
an old man burned beyond hope.
How could she clean such a one,
lay the white cloth over genitals
and scrub the scorched flesh?
The body washer's children would starve,
so she mumbled through the chosen
Koranic verses and knew that night
would hold visions of the dead.
Her calling came when a young mother
and her enfant were fused together
in a car fire. The body washer
got permission to clean them as one.
Since the American invasion,
work has been steady, too many
bodies to wash, despite the gifts
from their families. She teaches
her daughters the proper way
to clean the dead. There is little work
for poor girls. She would not have them
turn to prostitution. You must believe
in a strong hereafter, study the Koran,
and let the soul choose the verses to chant
as you scrub and herb the skin. At night
she still dreams of the mother and child
cauterized into one embrace, purified by fire.
You must prepare a white cloth to lay
the body on, and another one to cover it.
You must hold in your heart disparate verses
as if they were one. Dust, the only possession
death carries to the grave, is sprinkled
on the loved one's eyes.

The Language of Rain

How luxurious a forest after rain—
soft moss woven in the wreckage
of old wood, a gallery of lichen
on tree bark. It is winter—

beech trees cling to tattered leaves
to translate the language of rain,
to interpret wind. If you live among beech,
you keep something inside that listens

for that sound, that asks, did I hear it
when the fox stood at the mailbox,
or the day news pronounced the first
soldiers dead and flashed their pictures.

One morning I pulled a blanket around
my shoulders and sat on the porch to hear
rain and beech leaves make that sound.
What were they saying—nothing about

machine gun fire, sudden explosions,
burned-out markets, or a shoe
in the street still wearing a foot,
but something about the birth

of my neighbor's foal and the reflection
of the mare's eyes in the watering trough,
that between clapping leaves and scattered
rain there is a silence I long for.

With the Help of Birds

For to come upon warblers in early May
was to forget time and death.
   —*Theodore Roethke*

Every poem of death
   should start
with my mother's love
   for birds.
Finches and waxwings
   her favorites,
though she wasn't
   one to quibble;
an eagle dragging a carp
   across the sky
would do.

There are worse things
   than being dead.
You might be swallowed
   by the daily minutia
of the great mundane,
   to be spit up
years later
   wondering where
your life has gone.

But loving something
   can save you:
the way finches
   stack a feeder,
meddle in each other's
   business until
a woodpecker crashes in,
   littering surrounding
shrubs with wings.

Last summer my wife
    found a hummingbird
on Mount Pisgah.
    Its emerald wings trembled
as its feet tried to grasp
    her fingers.
A ranger said
    that their lives
are so short anyway.
    What a curious reply,
I thought, but later
    reconsidered.
Perhaps any time
    being a hummingbird
is enough.

Table Nine

Oh Grandmother,
while eating breakfast
at Cracker Barrel,
imagine my surprise
to find your antique picture
hanging in a grouping
with a Coca-Cola sign,
a stranger on a tractor,
and a mule breaking sod

You taught me
how to tight-line fish
on Cub Creek,
to spit on my hands,
and rub them in sand
to take an eel off a hook,
to steal eggs beneath a hen,
to suck on Hore Hound
to make it last.

Which cousin betrayed you,
hawked the portrait at a yard sale,
not knowing that you'd end up
in a chain restaurant
with an old-timer motif?

The last time our eyes met
you were in intensive care
at the Madison County Hospital,
hooked up to machines, your jaw
set against doctors who wouldn't
let your heart stop so you could
drift to your just reward.

Now you hang above table nine
in the non-smoking section,
honored or condemned,
I don't know, to gaze
at two eggs over-easy
with hash-browns. Rhonda
will be your server now.

Last Rite to the Queen of Grammar

Nothing dangled
when she walked into the room,
not lizards, not participles.
Slang split
but no infinitives.
And pronouns,
objective and subjective,
tap-danced warily
on our tongues.
The minister said,
in confidence,
that she would correct God,
and lawyers sought her out
for conversations.
Churchill would have cowered
behind her use of prepositions,
and Who and Whom felt comfortable
washing and drying supper dishes.
There were stories of how
her father wore his oldest tie
to rake the leaves,
and the mechanic at the ESSO
buttoned his shirt to fill
her tank once a week.
Though we joke about her
on holidays, we write
our checks out to the line,
never mix the second person,
tip precisely, drink scotch neat
on the right occasions,
and proof our children's
thank you notes for spelling.

It is true that we have been unthankful,
that we have been known
to drink white wine with beef,
waste food, curse machines,
and covet our neighbors,
but we don't enjoy it.

Winter Wind Song

    I only borrowed this dust.
            —*Stanley Kunitz*

The sound the wind makes
    circling winter's jagged porch
    is my father's long whistle
    when he called us home,

a blowing rock in a night storm,
    a mountain bald
    whispering to God,
    my grandmother's eerie lilt—

come—this—away—ka—tee
    as a panther lured
    a girl into the forest
    alone.

Some elemental sound
    still whistles in my dreams,
    wakes me wide-eyed—
    listening, listening

as snow moves in these many years.
    I try to keep the moment,
    stretch it in a solitude
    of lost faces, lost sounds

half hidden in the heart's
    mausoleum.
    There will come a time,
    the oracle says at story's start.

Perhaps that time has always been.
    This morning I welcome
    the circling sound
    of winter wind—

a whistle that no longer
    calls me home,
    I wake each morning
    who I am.

My Father Made Love

My father made love to failure.
The curve of his lips turned down
in timid sorrow, to men whose
promises meant little, whose
greed made love to nothing.

My father made love to my mother,
her shoulders, her feet, her hair.
He cherished the air she breathed,
the air that trailed her expectations,
unreached, unreachable.

My father made love to the shower
he crooned in, to the hymns he sang,
to the grape juice he served
as the blood of Jesus, his own
blood mortal and sick in love.

Oh, but cypress knees, birch bark,
arrowheads, igneous rock, tuned motors,
the ears of dogs were his lovers.
My father was the man who made love
to rivers, the Buffalo into the Duck

into the Tennessee. He spread their maps
on the floor and traced their flow
with fingers to read his future.
Cut bait, fishing line, sculling paddle,
the lugger cats he pulled from the water,

he made love to anything. My father
made love to camp sites, to tents he staked
and trenched against the coming rain
when his stars imploded, his mountains folded,
his rivers drown in a desk drawer.

My father died watching *Gunsmoke*,
died loving the carpet I laid him on,
the palms I used to pump his chest,
the lips I placed over his mouth.
His last breath was mine.

My Mother's Soul

My mother looked like a soul
waiting to be surprised. Whether
stirring soup or weeding a garden,
she was fishing for the unexpected,
like the morning at Reelfoot Lake
when her pole bent double,
and she swung a large water snake
swimming the air like a Chinese dragon.
She wouldn't just cut the line
and *throw away a perfectly good hook*,
so I pinned the snake's head,
threaded the barb from its lip,
and released it writhing
and scarred into cypress grass.

My mother wore a slight smile
that posed a question few people
wanted asked, especially the preacher
at Bible study, my sister on the phone,
or my brother sneaking in late
on Saturday night. A soul is what
she looked like until she died,
but forever is a concept I'll leave
to holy men on street corners
holding signs of coming doom.

Give me something concrete,
my mother might have said,
like a snake pumping a fishing line,
or an old woman sailing her death bed
toward the Rapture, her faith strong,
her face like a soul, the morphine "O"
of her mouth dark enough to swallow stars.

The News Inside

The News Inside

The news we hear is full of grief for that future,
but the real news inside here
is there's no news at all.

    —Rumi

        Rumi, the headline news
this morning is not new—a gunman enters a
fitness center and opens fire on an aerobics class
killing four.

        Surely someone should report
that a charitable person in every American city fed
breakfast to a homeless family.

        On my creek-walk this morning
an eastern kingbird eating a late summer hatch of flies
says the bugs are tasty.

        Early August rains inspire
the mock orange to bloom again, perfuming the nest
where the wrens have hatched their second brood.

        *Those apples grow from the Gift,
and sink back into the Gift*, you said. Rumi, what is
the *reedsong* in one heart worth?

        I swear I heard it this morning
in the sift of cottonwood leaves on Sulfur Fork, or in
my breath, or both.

        Tell me, who owns *that future*,
Old Sufi Mystic, knocking on both sides of the door?

The Melting

There should be hope in the leaves' first turning—
summer green fringed gold and crimson, webbed
hands reaching out against the curtain's blue.

Winter and what it takes from the heart
is almost worth it. Year by blessed year,
in the shortened days, something is stolen

that cannot be reclaimed—a swelling in the chest
when night comes soon. At a certain age
a man takes a season's beginnings, the small

beauties—frozen rings on creek rocks,
the first skein of ice in the horse trough.
He holds it to the morning sun and it burns

his palm as it drips through his fingers.
Each year he grips it tighter
to see his face melt in the fire.

Dark Fire

Driving down Walker Creek Road,
I carry the memory of a younger self
who admired the deep wooded hollow
and the gray tobacco barns. In early autumn,

dark-fire smoke drafted through roof vents
perfuming an October sky. It's New Year's,
and my father's memory curls in the bark
of yellow birch along the creek.

A neighbor's horses drink from a trough.
Water riddling from their big lips
catches the sun. Today, I notice
the names of roads anew—

Kelly Willis Road, Glenne Lea, Baker Station.
What's become of people who wore those names?
I marvel at how place is marked by names
whose memories have long since faded,

locked in some county vault filled
with unread records. I can't imagine
a road named Bill Brown.
I'd rather have my countenance

thought of as I think of my father
among the birches. Let my name
fade away with the lips of those who speak it
like the dark-fire smoke rising in fall.

Bookish

The books on the nightstand tire of being
added to when they've hardly been
touched, their pages crisp and unmarked,

their stories imprisoned, sentenced to be unlived.
In desperation they read my dreams instead—
the story of a boy whose character is never

quite developed, unable to make decisions,
uncomfortable in his own skin, obsessed
with the circumstances of his father's death—

Shakespeare did it better, they think.
And how desperately he adored his mother,
left alone with her during adolescence. *Sounds*

Oedipal, the book on Jung comments. It's all
been done before they agree, magical realism
with rabbit tricks: lazy student experiments

with drugs, becomes a poet, then a teacher,
how unoriginal, he must be impressed with
the Beats—I bet he's never been to San Francisco.

Sometimes their outrage wakes me. I tell my wife
to turn over and stop snoring. Other times I find them
rearranged, Stevens separated from Hemingway

to avoid a fistfight at Key West, Joyce and Marquez
in a jealous feud over narration. Several times my
water glass has been knocked off the table.

Tonight I turn in early, thumb through a *New Yorker*
 and read the comics. I notice *The Modern Poets*, teetering:
Ginsberg howls, Plath rants about her Daddy. Thomas urges

not to go gentle into that good night, Delmore Schwartz
says *The Heavy Bear That Goes With Me* is restless,
Frost thinks that I've got miles to go before I sleep.

Listening to Japanese Music at Starbucks, I Think of Basho

         How fitting, my old companion,
that while I drink iced coffee
I hear your words rise from memory.
Isn't it right that *The broom*
forgets about the snow. If it
lasts another year the broom
will know the snow again.
The spider forgets the crone
on the porch swing after she's gone,
and the wind will forget the spider once
the eggs are laid and flies are wrapped.

         You said, *Already I can see*
my own wind-bleached bones. I never
saw my bones, Basho, but I dreamed
my ashes dusting a mountainside,
or the decaying of flesh, a type
of combustion, my physics teacher said.
We are all burning, our matter waiting
to shape another form.

A cold wind cuts me,
you said. Yes, the burning gets frigid
as winters stack in the heart's storeroom.
I am cut too by your words—some things
centuries don't change and the detail
in experience means more than time.
Whatever mystery awaits, forgetfulness
and memory, like death, are stains
we can't remove.

Just butterflies
and sunlight, you said,
in the whole empty meadow.

Myotis Lucifugus

Second week in July, and Tennessee cornfields
grow thick with green swords that fence in the wind.
A storm brewing in the Gulf has sent thunderheads
thumbing up the Mississippi, and summer drought
is over for a time. Country church steeples spear the sky.
When I was a boy, I wanted to climb
into our church steeple and talk with God.
One Sunday I found the door unlocked
that hid the ladder. I worked my way up slowly,
terrified at my own curiosity. Instead of God,
I found a clapperless old bell, a smearing
of pigeon droppings, and a dead bat, which
I hid in my inside coat pocket to sneak home.
I sat on the family pew next to my mother,
thinking how mortified she would be
to know that I was taking Holy Communion
with a dead bat in my pocket. I swallowed the host
and remembered that it turned into the flesh of Jesus.
To make matters worse, the sermon was on angels.
A presence in my pocket pressed against my chest,
and I felt the bat's heart beat with mine.
At home, the encyclopedia said *Myotis Lucifugus*—
little brown bat. In secret, I buried it
in our animal cemetery with a turtle, a rabbit,
and two dogs. I spread its wings out one last
time and asked God to accept the steeple bat.
Fifty years later and I'm still talking to God,
usually when I'm driving alone looking
in the rear view mirror as if He were a child
in the back seat counting red barns.

Today I know that *Lucifugus* comes from Latin—
shunning the light. I think of the bat asleep
in the steeple that pointed toward heaven,
when all along paradise was flying in darkness
over the Forked Deer River, a gut full
of mosquitoes, a gift of summer rain.

Long Division

Walking beside Sulfur Fork Creek,
a great blue heron stalks the shallows,
the shapes of painted turtles rise,
and a queen snake suns on a rock.

I think of poor Adam and his job of naming.
Even in the Tennessee hills the task is endless.
What was Yahweh thinking?
Some of the names must have come easy—

swallowtail, luna moth, bluebird,
violet, hearts a busting. But every bacteria,
slime mold, lichen? Even the slider
slipping into the water keeps its promise

to thrive and multiply. In this magical world
of physics and chemistry—do the math—
divide backwards by any number
and never reach the zero in creation.

I would look up the exact scripture
but my wife is using my Bible
to press wild flowers—columbine,
anemone, flame azalea, larkspur.

The Appointment

It's hard to start every day anew,
the mind ragtag with sleep's phantoms

and daily habits as unavoidable
as cat litter. Why not be late for

your 9 o'clock with the committee?
Tell them you're sorry, but you stopped

to chaperone a tortoise crossing a road.
Tell them you couldn't ignore

the harbingers of spring—bloodroot,
hepatica, wild iris. Tell them tribal peoples

used bloodroot as an aphrodisiac,
spread blood-red dye on their faces.

Tell them Greeks used hepatica to heal
the liver, that an iris held to a cheek

feels as waxy sweet as a girl's ear.
Tell them that while mulching the garden

you found a ringneck snake, most private
of animals, its tiny necklace yellow

with new scales. Tell them that you
wish to renegotiate your travel plans,

extend your all-too-brief visit to this planet,
that you need time off to file your nails

so when you make love to your wife
you won't harm her perfect skin.

Wednesday Miracles

Driving down the ridge, I watch a meadow
of chicory shimmer in the breeze like a lake.

From a closer view, thistle and goldfinches
speckle the floral waves pink, black, and yellow.

Some mornings miracles dress themselves
like Renoir's little girl in blue. Today

I choose to believe in miracles—a flash
of indigo bunting in the sun, a child making faces

in a car window, while her mother argues on a cell,
throws me a kiss. I catch it and send it back.

On this Wednesday I'm forgiving everyone—
the mother on the phone, the truck that cut me off,

even the raucous crow that mocks forgiveness.
Like me, it knows we need more forgiveness

than we can gift. Shouldn't it be that way?
Humbled by desire to come clean, to finally

have it out with belief, we admit that belief
is perhaps worth the doubt it takes to get there,

and doubt involves a dangerous caring. But not
on a day of miracles when a field of chicory

becomes a mountain lake dressed in the hues
of Renoir's painting—a blue-clad girl

with golden hair absorbed in a book.
Who can't believe on a morning

when indigo buntings masquerade as sun gods
and a child throws a stranger her kiss.

The Names of Creeks

for James Still

Today the rounds of hay sit quietly in their fields.
A light frost melts from their tops, steams the air
like loaves of fresh bread on someone's porch.

The hills, like the heads of children sleeping,
are scruffed with hardwoods. They tangle
with huckleberry, like my morning heart,

not easy to sort through, pathless and mum.
Accept whatever comes, a great poet said. I want
to invert that thought: come to whatever accepts,

but the words don't make the right sense exactly.
Today sense nestles in the names of creeks:
Dry Fork, Crippled, Troublesome, New Hope.

Indigo

> The light which dwells in our words...
> —*Jeff Hardin*

One can hear the river in a poem,
feel the tug of forever as the moon
glints the shoals, the current constant,
the light changing interpretation as
the planet moves. The light on a bunting's

wing becomes the word bunting
and will always be that light, half
bluebird, half sun god. Indico, from
Spanish, from Latin, indicum, from
Greek, indikon, *Indian* (dye),from Indikos.

How far can you trace a color in language,
the same timeless sun bouncing off
feathers as they flutter across the road?
The word, *mother*, she who first
pointed out the bird feeding in river grass,

will always be part of that name,
her face visiting dreams years after
her death. So say the word *bunting*
and indigo will follow and the memory
of the one who taught this bird

at the edge of the river where the sun
still bounces off a roll of shoals, where
a person might come to reclaim a part
of the self, in hopes that the light which
dwells in words in some way dwells in us.

Journey

> I have traveled widely in Concord...
> —Thoreau

Through the leaf-strewn yard of autumn—
oak, hickory and sweet gum, maple and persimmon—
I hear roughly the same hush under boot,

and the snap of dry twigs. Because my home
is on the ridge top, I drive through the hills
that follow Sulfur Fork, greet turkey and deer,

speak kindly to the old black lab
who sleeps in the road by her barn.
I've stopped to watch a kestrel, copper

and gray sentinel, scour a field for mice.
I've read the pecking order of buzzards
feeding on a doe's belly, studied how

they tear the rich viscera, then hop
and squawk with a relish of joy.
I've seen children tour an ancient cemetery,

reading epitaphs and names. I've studied
grave diggers, shoulder deep in soil,
shoring up a shadowed grave as an egret

fished a hilltop pond, as dusk drown
the sun in a scurry of mauve. Follow
the sycamore leaf's downward spiral

and learn of the heart's meter,
that in an average life it echoes
two and half billion beats. How long

I failed to heed what childhood taught me—
the slowing of the pulse as night comes on,
the sound of the earth beneath my feet.

Elemental

The Way

> As you start to walk out on the way, the way appears...
> —*Rumi*

The path that led to your childhood creek
was always new. A rabbit, a tortoise, a ribbon snake—
your direction altered by wonder.
There was no test on where you ended up.
It wasn't about how to climb a tree,
but which tree looked lonely without you—
the maple with fall red leaves,
the natural ladder of magnolia limbs,
the creek birch where hummingbirds waited.
The child inside amazed, unstructured time
a blessing—you're lost already if you
know your destination. Pick a day
when rain dots a window, clouds hug treetops,
a day when you'd like to carry a blanket
over your shoulders like a boy playing Superman.
Let the cat out, let yourself out, time doesn't wait
like a set clock. Bless the porch rocker that rocks
empty in a storm. Bless the armrests that invite
small hands to grip cracked paint, bless the worn
and faded, how comfort comes with old things.
Bless a journey without legs; no need to stand
when eyes walk the forest edge. Bless shadows
trees make when sunlight breaks through
rain clouds. Bless the small accidents of the world—
the barn mow hole weathered into a crooked smile.
Bless the barred owl that lives in the rafters,
and the nightly journey of hunger and death
when its way appears.

The Light That Follows Rivers

Like the light that follows rivers in the night,
    a figure hovers ghostlike in my dreams,
my father or stranger, sometimes the same,
    his blue eyes stained, his thoughts to read.

His gruff hands hover luminous in my dreams,
    above my childhood slumber they touch my head.
His blue eyes like his hands I wish to read—
    yet I am older than my father when he died.

Above my childhood slumber they touched my head—
    his eyes, his hands, his storied voice, all lullabies.
Though I am older than my father when he died,
    as men we travel alone, I know that now.

His eyes, his hands, his storied voice, his lullabies,
    my father, my stranger, always the same—
as men we travel lonely, I know that now,
    like the light that follows rivers in my dreams.

The Bells

Small bells toll childhood's wooden chimes—
   my father's humble laughter,
      the clink of bottles left by milkmen—
         all in another century.
Yet dogs still bark at strangers,
   cats yowl in the thicket,
      and mockingbirds defend
         their plots with stolen syllables.
At my age, what isn't stolen?
   Sixty years of keepsakes
      archived in the heart's hockshop.
         Closed during the day,
it opens at night—
   but nothing's for sale,
      just a gallery of faces, places,
         lost emotions wound
into stories—
   how myth invades
      our private lives—
         the rough fingers
of a father's gentle touch,
   a mother's honest demands
      for honest deeds,
         flash of guilt—
has something broken?
   My boyhood friend
      pulls his jeep
         on a gravel road
and we piss the beer
   my brother bought us—
      my friend dead
         these many years,
his face bright, his future
   all his parents wanted,
      this presence in my dream.

Elemental

I.

On the Tellico River, rocks that shape
the water's flow grow smooth and undercut
by this myriad force. At night, shadowed
by sycamore and birch, wherever current
brushes stone, shivers a glow. Light
from distant stars and our squat moon shimmers
Bald River Falls, perhaps tricks natural
selection and our mammalian optic nerve
to accept this magic as just an evening
beside a mountain stream the Cherokee
claim as holy.

II.

Memory changes the narrative:
my grandmother teaching me
how to tight-line fish without a cork.
It's in the feel of the pole, the line tension—
what's in the water on the other end,
the slight lift of wrist when the jerk comes,
all with early willow green, how it can't
be separated in the moment—the elements—
stone outcrop, light in trees, the river—
how an old woman made of flesh commands
such resolve—flesh, mostly water, mineral—
light and shadow, brushstrokes in the eyes,
nuance of voice. My father loved rivers
as much as Jesus—the Buffalo, the Duck,
the Caney Fork, the Tennessee, time there,
earthly sacraments of something he knew eternal.
Why so much hoodoo about heaven
when the river and this life demand our praise.

III.

River, how rain pocks your moving surface—
little rings swirling just enough to confuse
the clouds as tall reeds at your bank form
green sleeves. And how polished rocks
beneath the shoals sing for you.
My wife cracked the windows, and your
breeze-song entered sleep like camphor,
as if night held seashells to our ears.
You are blind to what my eyes gather
from your surface, and yet I use
the second person as if you understood
my syllabic babble. But you speak a language
old as stone. I sit on your bank and glimpse
the everlasting, as a moon rises red
through dark limbs, turns yellow, and brightens
eddy and current swirl—a moon you can draw
water from, its lunar drift in every pail.

Flying

We boarded the john boat to explore
the myriad collage of river—light, water,
wind, birds, smell of dead fish, and broken
mussel shells, their mother of pearl
bejeweled along the river's edge.

Great stone bluffs above the far shore held
my grandmother's stories of caves,
rattlesnakes, and the dead—always the dead—
and how the bluffs were willed to spirits
that chose to stay. This is what my thoughts
turned to—mysteries that shaped questions
a boy might ask: Why would hunters
take refuge in a cave filled with serpents?
Why would Indians chase a young woman
off a cliff? And what if a boy staring down
from the high bluff leapt from his brother's arms
and for a moment knew what the woman knew
before she was broken on the rocky shore?

Perhaps that night a tolerant God let him
dream of flying, even soaring above trees
to reach the sun, before the quick heart-
fall into, not the river, nor the shore,
but the cabin floor beneath the bunk bed,
his knees scraped, cheeks bruised blue,
his pulse too desperate for words.

Off Shore

Remember how Mother asked our father
to kill a water moccasin at the edge
of Reelfoot Lake? Cautious and deliberate,
with reasons he couldn't deny, though
he hated death, had seen too much of it,
at home and on a battleship in the Pacific.
He didn't care to kill anything;
the snake wasn't intruding, living
its life in its home. But he fashioned
a large stick into a club, then bludgeoned
the serpent that coiled on a log. Night
masked his face—the night I came to recognize.
Why couldn't we move the picnic,
my sister asked, but the deed was done,
and the snake flung like a chain
into open water beyond cypress knees.
We built a fire to appease the gods.
Hotdogs and buns lay in their packages
as evening closed tight around
our tiny spot on the planet, closed
like a constrictor. The sounds
of frogs and night birds rose
against something just off shore
that in years to come resembled
my father's face.

Rare

Even in a world where silence is rare,
I come to this bridge to hear creek water

drift through a line of sycamores.
I kneel beside the oldest tree, where

life has carved a dark hollow the length
of its trunk, listen to wind whistle

its death like a flute, and watch branches,
great white hands finger the sky.

Fiddleheads cling to roots that reach
in the creek, forming little caves for perch.

A lover of trees, my mother stopped the car
near sycamores to study the strange art

of splotched bark, as if each tree might map
some distant universe. Overhead, a heron

floats to fish the evening shift, drifts without
moving wing to the limestone shore.

I place my hand inside the hollow, rub the scars—
I know something is eating us all, come to love

the dark gnawing and the power it brings.
Too late for shadows, the sun fallen

behind ridge, world itself becomes shadow,
enough to silence the kingfisher and send

her toward home, sound of creek searching
rock and eddy, silhouette of limbs

scratching an evening sky, enough
to send me on my slow walk home as well.

Savor

> We have a soul at times...
> —Wistawa Szymborska

which means at times we don't.
We weave our lives at times;
at times our lives are woven for us.

      Not woolen threads as our mothers
might have it, or cotton, but rayon,
unborn, electric, sticking to our flesh like August.

      Not August gold with drought-burned
corn, but glass and concrete angling the sky
away from grass and bone.

At times a soul claims us
like a lake claims the moon,
wobbles it, stretches it—
God's lamp
          lighting our names
toward home—my father's supper whistle
that brought us racing behind our spaniel,
Wags—the smell of fresh soup
permeating our back porch like marrow.

We knew even then
          the delight
hunger makes when sated,
how the soul chooses hunger
over plenty
         because plenty has
so little to follow, and our bread
sopped the last rich savor before
we pled for more.

Singularities

> The holy singularities of this now uncommon day...
> —*C. K. Williams*

While we were gone, the October garden sprouted
ghost stalks and frost-scorched vines—
the neighbor cast bruised tomatoes
across the road to feed the hog. Migrant doves
gleaned the vestiges of corn and beans,

a season's vestments to thatch winter soil.
It is human to make a fall day sacrament—
even rot and decay, the god of entropy,
earth tilting as it parades around a star—
all reasons to worship—if you're warm,

fed, and know a dry place to sleep and read.
A flock of waxwings come to harvest
juniper berries, drink in unison
at the metal pot. Their cricket voices season the air.
I have searched for you, even as you shred

hornet's nest and plant fiber, churned with dye,
to make textured paper—how you lose
yourself to discover something new.
On this uncommon day, three Sandhill cranes
stop to rest upon crown above the orchard.

Your green eyes follow their shadows
as you tuck blond curls behind your ear, trailing
a crimson stain on your neck. Winter's knife
is rusty, yet to be whetted by ice and wind,
but something's always coming at fall's end.

So I sharpen its blade with memory—
how I kissed my father's forehead in that
sudden death room, how I held Mother's
small hands, how I woke in an old motel
on a mountain morning to caress you.

Rearview

Sometimes he looks in the rearview mirror
and sees the old cat standing at the mailbox

with his wife—the cat that stays after it dies,
the wife who doesn't age, her blond curls draping

her chin like soft curtains, as she sits
on the porch steps smiling at the grand

pumpkin she grew that won second prize
at the fair. The straps of her worn overalls

hug her shoulders the way he wished
his arms could drape around her neck, nose

buried in the hair next to her ear, her smell,
orchard fresh, peach or apple or plum.

He loved the way she yelled *look* the time
she pointed at Sandhill cranes circling

the hill above the house and landed, but
he was watching her dance like a ballerina

in garden shorts, hands reaching
at the sky. Now the past circles like ancient

birds and never quite lands where expected,
the orchard dozed by the next owner,

top of the hill a white barn instead
of a pasture crown. A blue pickup emerges

in the mirror, the driver raises two fingers
from the steering wheel, passes on the right.

Mauve

for Jenny

The silence beneath our words
is often defining, perhaps what
color means in music. Mauve,
your mother's favorite,
a complexity hard to lift
from a palette, shade only
the sky can truly paint.
So say *mauve* and a silence
reaches your mother's dementia.

Her two paintings emerge—
one of a Vermont sunset,
the other, Gulf surf just before dark.
They hang in our house, old friends
that never quite reached her un-
reachable goal—a farmhouse
surrounded by Green Mountains
and the last shade on the horizon
glossing a roll of waves.

I pray your mother dreams
mauve until the sky liberates her
from the nursing home,
lifts her spirit up and we can
cast her ashes out to sea.

And so the word *mauve*, spoken,
becomes an old lady strapped in a bed,
becomes two paintings, becomes
prayer, and a word that must be
said to complete the silence.

My Wife's Tattoo

It's the Japanese symbol for heron,
needled into her inside wrist, that

most delicate of skin—a place some
people slit, but for her, an ancient bird

that stalks the shallows, its stillness
and shape, the envy of art.

I have watched them wade creek current,
stalk a Gulf beach at mid-night,

and once at Reelfoot Lake, a great blue
caught a snake that coiled the heron's neck

to keep from being swallowed. They
battled for an hour until, exhausted,

both released. My wife says that on a day
when self is unconscious of self,

a heron's sudden appearance in a setting
invades like a memory, unresolved.

It must be studied until a stabbing beak breaks
the water's surface with sometimes an answer.

Magic

I remember the sun rising like Lazarus—
dead so long, shocked by its own brightness.
I am thinking about the crow in its maple
at road's edge, how he greets me
when I pass, how he curses each blessed
day with his raucous praise.

My boyhood friend lies emaciated and dying;
there have been times when death stayed mute,
the news blotted out by choice. This morning
crow whispers with the wind, and the hooded
shadow invades a day as ordinary as a dying star
or a fist-size muscle stopping.

As teens, we visited a fortune teller to find out
whom to love. Today the tarot shadows
the kitchen table, but the wands can't trump
the last card. The past invades like a beggar,
tin cup outstretched.

Memory returns to Reelfoot Lake
when a storm forced us to wade the snake-ridden
swamp and drag the john boat to Green Island.
A twister formed a water spout of tangled trees.
Ship burned a leech off my ankle with
his cigarette. He always saved my ass
from something, even if he had to conjure it.

Today Magic can't pull a rabbit from a hat
or raise the dead. Nothing rises but the yard crow
and the past, and I bless the stars for both.

Applesauce

The last of the Arkansas Blacks
were too high for deer, and my mother,
visiting, wouldn't have them wasted—
so I climbed a ladder high into branches,
pillowcase in hand, gathered those I could reach
and shook others into soft autumn grass.

        The sky,
an October blue, pointed toward
shorter days. The fruit weren't pretty—
spotted with cedar rust, wasp cratered.
Her determined hands, as splotched
as fruit, peeled on the porch 'til
they were done. She sliced and boiled
them to mush, added brown sugar,
lemon juice, and my mother's pièce
de résistance, fresh vanilla, to distinguish
hers from all the rest.

           This spring morning,
despite a light frost, the old tree burns
white with new blossoms. Mother's
smudged canning apron bleached clean
and folded in a drawer, her busy shadow
gone from the kitchen these many months.
No visits left in this life, except her lesson
about waste, the importance of making
much out of little, the memory of a steamed
kitchen scented with vanilla, and one jar
left in the pantry no one will touch.

Tortoise Morning

> Even the poorest thing shines.
> —*Layman P'ang*

Today my identity will remain as nameless
as the given name of the tortoise grubbing

my garden. Its shell catches the sun,
sends my eyes an orange not quite

any other orange, an orange Gauguin
might have burnished as an idea of beauty.

It holds a piece of lettuce in its mouth
like a geisha's fan and chews slowly,

fanning the zinnias, the little kabuki.
Maple leaves drip from last night's storm,

a type of silence one can hear, like
snowfall in a forest, a silence that

makes you aware of the silence that is.
Even the crow perched on the fence post

whispers to the mustang something about
the way the pasture smells after rain,

word that can only be spoken in crow.
Perhaps being nameless sharpens the senses

when the sun rainbows blades of grass
and morning's an infant too young to speak.

Start with a Bad Memory—

    your father's dead blue eyes
        stare at the ceiling,
the doctor hovers over him,
    stethoscope probing his chest
        like a vacuum cleaner,
but there's nothing left
    to retrieve except
        spittle on his chin.

Now, a few questions—
    why write poems thirty years
        later about this same event?
Death has enough power.
    Why not remember
        the bonfire builder,
man at whose feet
    dogs worshiped,
        the shower
 resounding his tenor,
    I'll fly away in the morning,
        tenderness of his callused hands?

And your mother's screams—
    crying out to God—
        let's say they were operatic,
mythic—Leda, for instance, or Icarus;
    Prometheus and his liver ailment
        for sneaking fire to man.

Now picture a fire grate
   in the upstairs
      bedroom,
   how the night before his death
      they held hands
and poked socked feet
   through flannel pajamas,
      blue coals sparkling their eyes.

Something Like Grace

> My religion makes no sense
> and does not help me
> therefore I pursue it...
> —Anne Carson

I was taught that God dwelled close
enough to drag my open fingers
through the air of Him,
particles adrift with holy energy
blessing the hearts of hungry
children and demented souls
in nursing homes—praise them.

I was taught to pray for my enemies—
terrorists, bigots, bullies, and investors
who grow rich off the working poor—
praise them.

And especially praise be to columbine,
star grass, and iris which return in my
garden each spring like miracles, nudged
with 10-10-10 that dissolves into moist soil,
brought by sacred rain—praise them.

And children's small hands, busy
in wonder of their senses—may
they investigate all that doesn't harm—
may tiny creatures they study live
without injury.

Thanks be to April and October
for birthing what I love and
to January and August for teaching
me to tolerate what I don't.

Creator of small industries—
ants trucking leaf bits toward holes,
bees dancing honeysuckle maps,
homeless collecting aluminum cans
from roadside ditches—praise them,
praise them all.

And praise to dark matter that holds
the universe together and tears apart—
and to night windows, first light
and clumsy hands that reach
beyond themselves.

Driving the County

The road leads beside Cross Creek,
where shade from fall leaves,
maple and sycamore,

blinks light on water and stone,
as the sun spins earth on its journey,
and dark matter swells cosmic gravity—

always in flux like fields of starlings
combing for seeds amidst broom sage
and timothy. An ancient mound rises

above Indian Grave Point Cave,
entry to the afterlife in another time.
This earthy swell, worn by centuries,

is part of the mystery our footsteps tread
before they are blown clean or washed
in the creek with its burble and light.

The word *Father* emerges in prayer,
habit learned in childhood, my father
dead some 47 years, just a pinch of sand

in the desert. Time like the energy
in matter drags creation forward.
I could say *Mother* instead, and another

constellation is lit—say *sister*, say *brother*,
say *wife*, say *work* and the circle
of a man's life from birth to now

appears like asters in late fall,
vibrant as a brush stroke of purple
to dapple the autumn swell.

Acknowledgments

NEW POEMS

Grateful acknowledgment is made to editors of the following publications in which some of these poems first appeared, sometimes in different forms:

Aurorean: "Mountain Morning with Deer"

Big Muddy: "Why We Display the Broken"

Birmingham Poetry Review: "Vestment"

Cloudbank Poetry Review: "Breathe in Four," "Letter to October"

Clover: A Literary Rag: "How We Think It Must Have Been," "Portent"

Cumberland River Review: "When the Boy Leaves the River"

Jimson Weed Review: "Early Spring Prayer," "This, Her Art"

Kindofahurricane Press Anthology on Secrets and Dreams: "Copperhead Dreams"

Kindred: "Sky and Soil," "Tortoise Shell"

POEM: "The Cairn," "Fall Passover," "In the Church of January," "On Finding My Father's Pocketknife in an Old Bag of Keys"

Still: The Journal: "In Praise of Drought," "Vespers"

Tar River Poetry: "This Morning"

SELECTED POEMS

The author wishes to offer profound thanks to the publishers of previously published books: *Holding On By Letting Go*, Bucksnort Press, 1986; *What the Night Told Me*, Mellen Press, 1992; *The Art of Dying*, Sow's Ear Press, 1996; *Gods of Little Pleasures*, Sow's Ear Press, 2001; *Yesterday's Hay*, Pudding House Press, 2005; *Tatters*, March Street Press, 2007; *Late Winter*, Iris Press, 2008; *The News Inside*, Iris Press, 2010; *Elemental*, 3: A Taos Press, 2014.

One or more poems from the selected sections first appeared in the following publications:

Appalachian Heritage . Art Life . Atlanta Review . Aurorean . Borderlands: Texas Poetry Review . Cloudbank . Connecticut Poetry Review . Cold Mountain Review . Cumberland Poetry Review . Diner . Dos Passos Review . Hamilton Stone Review . Homeworks: A Book of Tennessee Writers . Icon . Karamu . Medaphors . Motif: Anthology on Chance . Negative Capability . Now and Then . Passages North . Pikestaff Forum . Potomac Review . POEM . Prairie Schooner . Rambler Magazine . Raven Chronicles . Red Rock Review . Smartish Pace . South Dakota Review . Southern Poetry Review . Sou'Wester . Sow's Ear Poetry Review . Still: The Journal . Tar River Poetry . Tennessee English Journal . The Broad River Review . The Literary Review . West Branch . White Pelican Review . Windless Orchard . Witnessing Earth

About The Author

Bill Brown holds a degree in history from Bethel College and graduate degrees in English from the Bread Loaf School of English, Middlebury College, and George Peabody College. He is the author of ten poetry collections and a writing textbook on which he collaborated with Malcolm Glass. During the past thirty years, he has published hundreds of poems and articles in college journals, magazines, and anthologies. In 1999, Brown wrote and co-produced the Instructional Television Series, *Student Centered Learning,* for Nashville Public Television. Starting in 1983, Brown directed the writing program at Hume-Fogg Academic Magnet School in Nashville for nineteen years. He retired from Hume-Fogg in May, 2003 and accepted a part-time lecturer's position at Peabody College of Vanderbilt University. In 1995, the National Foundation for Advancement in the Arts named him Distinguished Teacher in the Arts. Brown has been a Scholar in Poetry at the Bread Loaf Writers Conference, a Fellow at the Virginia Center for the Creative Arts, and a two-time recipient of fellowships in poetry from the Tennessee Arts Commission. In 2011, the Tennessee Writers Alliance awarded Brown Writer of the Year. He and his wife Suzanne live in the hills of Robertson County with a tribe of cats.

Also by 3: A Taos Press

Collecting Life: Poets on Objects Known and Imagined – Madelyn Garner and Andrea Watson

Seven – *Sheryl Luna*

The Luminosity – *Bonnie Rose Marcus*

Trembling in the Bones: A Commemorative Edition – *Eleanor Swanson*

3 A.M. – *Phyllis Hotch*

Ears of Corn: Listen – *Max Early*

Elemental – *Bill Brown*

Rootwork – *Veronica Golos*

Farolito – *Karen S. Córdova*

Godwit – *Eva Hooker*

The Ledgerbook – *William S. Barnes*

The Mistress – *Catherine Strisik*

Library Of Small Happiness – *Leslie Ullman*

Day of Clean Brightness – *Jane Lin*

Bloodline – *Radha Marcum*

Hum of Our Blood – *Madelyn Garner*

Dark Ladies & Other Avatars – *Joan Roberta Ryan*

The Doctor of Flowers – *Rachel Blum*

Bird Forgiveness – *Melinda Palacio*

Turquoise Door – *Lauren Camp*